WITH MY HEAD RISING OUT OF THE WATER

poems by
John J. Brugaletta

Certain poems in this collection first appeared, sometimes in slightly different versions, in the following publications:

Relief, Blue Collar Review, Cyclamens and Swords, Legends, Zingara, Beyond the Pillars, Red River Review, Cahoodaloodaling, The Random House Treasury of Light Verse, and *Cowboy Poetry Press.*

A sincere thank-you to my wife and primary editor, Claudia McDonald Brugaletta.

With My Head Rising Out of the Water

poems by
John Brugaletta

A Negative Capability Press Book

Published in the United States of America by
Negative Capability Press
Mobile, Alabama

No part of the publication may be reproduced, scanned, stored or transmitted in any form, including all electronic and print media, or otherwise used without the prior written consent of the publisher.

Production & Design by HTDesignS

Printed in the United States of America

Text Copyright © 2014 by John J. Brugaletta

ISBN 9780942544862
LCCN 2014932098

Scan to visit
www.negativecapabilitypress.org

Scan to visit and like
Negative Capability on Facebook

Table of Contents

1. Voices on the Bus

- 3   *Caboose*
- 4   *A Brief Biography*
- 5   *A Barn Too Old*
- 6   *Courage and Cowardice*
- 7   *Artemis*
- 9   *Another Case at the Questura*
- 10   *Cassandra Takes the Podium*
- 12   *Coffee Shops*
- 13   *Philia Divided*

2. Some Days

- 17   *Cathartes*
- 18   *Fortune*
- 19   *Evolution Coming*
- 20   *Remembering Victory*
- 21   *Watching Water*
- 22   *Righteous Man*
- 23   *A Different Beginning*
- 24   *Everything Is Otherwise*
- 25   *The 20th Century*
- 27   *Rising Again*

3. The World Beside Us

- 31   *The Wolf People*
- 33   *Animal Script*
- 34   *Triptych*

Table of Contents *Continued*

- 35   *Barn*
- 36   *Trading and Breeding*
- 37   *Monkey See, Monkey Do*
- 38   *Exposed*
- 39   *May in the Garden*
- 40   *Extensions of the Body*
- 41   *Itadaki Masu*

4. Portraits

- 45   *Arthur on Lancelot*
- 46   *The Nurse in the Odyssey*
- 47   *Casual Chic*
- 48   *Apples on Snow*
- 50   *Autobiography*
- 51   *This Is Not a Marriage*
- 52   *Fishing Simplified*
- 53   *The Good Life*
- 54   *Aged*
- 55   *The Miser's Deadline*
- 56   *Thanksgiving*
- 57   *Being Alive and Having to Die*

5. Making Light of It

- 61   *The Woman Who Lived Backwards*
- 63   *Nasty Nick and the Banker's Kinfolk*
- 65   *Confession to Proclivities*

With My Head Rising Out of the Water

1. Voices on the Bus

CABOOSE

Imagine you are five, so when you sit
some frigid morning at the big oak table
spooning oatmeal in your mouth you see,
just above the window sill, a train.
But you've looked up too late to see the black
and puffing locomotive or its mate
the coal car. All you glimpse are late discipled
cars and, closest kin, toddling after,
that hard-put little brother the caboose.

The raisins in your oatmeal speak to you
of cottontails that skittered off, leaving
raisins on the snow, a simple-minded
scribe who's learned to write one word, his name.
You ask yourself why brothers run away.
It's the kind of question that expects
no answer, at least no satisfying one.
You're different, that's the thing, and no amount
of loving can repair or harmonize
the dissonance that marks you as a freak.

You're still imagining, but now you're old,
and now you realize that everyone's
a freak, everyone is left to eat
alone, catching sight of distant trains
too late — too late, and just in time for you.

A BRIEF BIOGRAPHY

Having gone through Okinawa's hell,
he wanted nothing more than work,
a wife, a little house, some kids,
a backyard for them to play in.

He learned to make Oldsmobiles run right
when they rattled or coughed or wouldn't start.
He still had foxhole nightmares,
swung his arms like fighting in his sleep.

But every weekday morning she would
pack his lunch, and he would proudly
drive to work, to the camaraderie,
to motor oil's smell, to jobs well done.

The only thing that bothered him was
feeding five children on what he made,
not on what he earned. It never struck him
that the boss had overpaid himself.

A BARN TOO OLD

A barn is dying of neglect and time
a mile or so away,
more openings to wind and rain and sleet
than boards against the day.

The farmer's moved his rattling, rusted truck
from crushing's huge collapse;
the feral cats have found a safer place
to take their feline naps.

I go by once each day and watch the slow
combustion of the will
his father had when he nailed board to plank,
and many young have still.

But I can only feel what has to be
when living's light goes dim,
to have no urge to mend or plant or sing —
a half-dead, unpruned limb.

COURAGE AND COWARDICE

That corporal never volunteered for anything.
When I asked him why,
he said because he was afraid.
But when the gunny told him
he would run recon patrol that night, he went,
brought back a ton of info
on enemy emplacements.

Morning came.
The captain ordered him to lead
a flank attack on their artillery
with half a dozen men.
They went. One marine survived to say
the corporal told the rest
to stay behind him as he ran uphill.
He took rifle fire in a lung and in his stomach
but kept going until a machine gun
sawed him in half.

We took the hill a few days later,
but just because we remembered one corporal
who fought back his fear.
We all were cowards
but we got things done.

ARTEMIS

On Crete, before the savage Greeks arrived,
I was the Lady of Wild Things. In Phrygia
I was Cybele. Ephesus was later, but I still
was mother goddess, as my many paps attested.
Only the Greeks, randy for boys and girls,
could give me paltry sacrifices as a virgin.

So when Agamemnon boasted that
his hunting skills could easily equal my own,
it was a tidy step to plot the death
of his most prized and virgin daughter.
He needed winds to carry his fat fleet to Ilium,
winds that would avenge the ravaged honor
of his bested brother, winds that I reversed,
sequestered and confused. Let him hunt
for ways to put a thousand ships
on Troy's windblown and flatland beach,
hunter that he boasts of when there's peace.

The oracle sat her tripod, went entranced,
and I sent mumblings of my target trade:
a simple sacrifice to bring fair winds Troyward,
and for no more than one daughter, Iphigeneia.
Then Calchas interpreted these mutterings.

The king, this son of lies, would have a choice
stewed in futility, ignominy at his impotence
to move the ships, or in the end be drained

of lifeblood by maddened Clytemnestra,
made murderous by mother-love.

And so the richest Greek, this mulish Mycenean,
snared in his royal robe, would be chopped down
like a tree by his wife's ax, and she herself
then murdered by her son, pleading with
her udders hanging out for mercy of her
bladed boy. And this it took, all this to calm
my anger at the Greeks, especially the family
of Atreus, for bullying my worshipers into
belief that I, so fertile once, am childless virgin
scouring the parched hills for pigs and deer
like some ragged beggar with a clumsy spear.

ANOTHER CASE AT THE QUESTURA

Each one had lost his precious body's red.
Brunetti wondered how they were alike.
And when the Transylvanians were brought in,
two cowboys asked, "Who are those guys?" and ran.

The father of one victim came to see
if his own son had spent his vital blood —
exclaimed, "Look how they drained my boy of blood."

The signorina, at her laptop, sighed;
her chores were not elettrica that day.
And in the doorway lurked Brunetti's bulk,
his eyes on her decolletage, which showed
more than his Paola could offer him
to keep his thoughts abreast of all the clues
and on the noble task of finding thugs.

CASSANDRA TAKES THE PODIUM

What good is fending off a lustful god
if all it brings is rape and slavery?
No hint of those stephanic blooms that grace
the heads of skillful whores. I will admit
I led him on to think that for the gift
of prophesy I'd lend him all I'd kept
in tight-wrapped robes. My yearnings were to be
a Sibyl, to reveal the absolute
while keeping me inviolate of men.
But when I'd been filled up with seer's skills
Apollo visited, stood by my bed.
I knew he'd come to have his pay: myself.
But I said, "Sibyls babble senseless truths,
a sign that they must never bear a child,
who would in time speak living sense and clear."

This scheme unmanned his full rigidity
and he, deflated, crept his chidden way.
It was not till I knew that Paris was
to be the torch that razed the ashlar walls
of Ilium that I could see the price
Apollo seized: once gargled out, the truth
translated, Alexandrus still unstained,
I'd be no more believed than those insane.
In fact they called me so. And then when I
perceived the wooden horse was pregnant with
a troop of Greeks, a handful seconded,
the mass of Trojans saying, "Take the gift."

It was the second time my second sight
had seen invisibly the fall of Troy,
and neither was believed. As for my prim
virginity, small Ajax conquered it
by forcing me from sanctuary's bay.
And that sweet desecration of Athena's
sanctity will bring ordeals on Greeks.
May that avenge the loss of Ilium.

But I would keep my purest days today
if rank Apollo sought my bed again.
For nothing good can last, not civic pride,
or cities saved by swapping sex for gifts,
or sacred longing for a truthful life.

COFFEE SHOPS

We stop at them on the roadside,
walk in and are relieved
that the chairs are plastic, the tables Formica,
everything orange and brown and scratched,
secure in their anachronism and imperfections,
like monks, or politeness.

The meringue on the pies
and the waitress's hair
both achieve height and elegance
by means of daily necessity.

The atmosphere is not ambience.
It is the honest flatulence of grease,
with high notes of potatoes and bacon.

The newspaper has been read
by someone who left
ten minutes ago for work.
It lies now despoiled,
as open to us
as a woman who has decided
anyone may know her without paying.

And the imitation flowers
do their best to mime
their evanescent betters.

We always have stopped at shrines like these
for a rest, or because we're hungry.

PHILIA DIVIDED

His knowledge masterful, his manner smooth,
his sense of humor quick as fingernails,
he made allowances for me when I
displayed my naiveté for all to see.

And so we were a pair of colleagues who
could share a joke or sack lunch in the lounge.

Because the two of us were of an age,
we both retired at the milennium,
I straight to redwoods on the northern coast
and he remaining gaily in the south,
a separation well designed to split
our sight, together with our genial minds.

But then the telephone began to chime
and, he in sun, I in the greening rain,
collegiality began to grow
into the sort of friendship that can last,
the taste for language that can taste the words
and bridge the gap dividing everyone.

2. some days

CATHARTES

You there, turkey buzzard circling,
goitered mortician in a black suit
and naked of necktie, head rotating
to spy or sniff out the dead or dying
in your daily quest to cleanse
this pasture and the world of corpses.

Unbeautiful neatener,
throat a vacuum hose ingesting
the flesh of lives spent or cut off,
then depositing it where it
will nourish both locoweed
and buttercups, I canonize you
Saint Charon of the birds.

FORTUNE

It was a comfort not to be the Czar.
Each summer he believed would be his last,
but people took him as a lowly tar.

Still, he believed each June would be his last,
that he was sinking like his native star,
for he had had his birthright's fortune cast.

Once cast, one's horoscopic future can't be far,
and it was comforting to not be Czar,
although some things were well about the past.

His headache was that rank iconoclast
who made him think each summer was his last.
He tensed to hear the tires of a car.

And then one day, at her due time, the char
said, "Run away. They come." He was aghast.
He took his pistol, doused his cheap cigar,

then ran. The cleaning woman heard a blast.
At that same time he dreamed of caviar
and richly furnished rooms, sweet smelling, vast.

EVOLUTION COMING

If sanity relies on landscapes of forgetfulness,
insanity must be an endless cloud of midges,
each one a sentence far too panic stricken
to wait and speak. What becomes a blur
is either decoration or desecration,
scroll work from a catalogue and
glued to someone's hairy back.
Is this the fabled end of all?
I think it's not, not yet.
But ages come as
newborns do,
with pain.

Perhaps,
as we evolve,
our hubris will
decline as we earn
a more efficient brain.
Maybe we will recognize
more midges as they speed
past our inner eyes on missions
we still won't comprehend or sense.
Then we will know and speak the parts
while still happily ignorant of the purposes,
which will make us about as good as we can get.

REMEMBERING VICTORY

Something named Victor makes a little trap
that holds a dab of peanut butter till
a mouse trots up to eat and it goes Snap
according to my wish and Victor's will.

The murder is committed late at night
when owls are hunting for this pint-sized bum.
He would have made one a sustaining bite,
not crushed by Victor's wood-and-wire chum.

He and his buddies chew my speakers' wires
and drop their scat wherever they can run.
I'm pleased to let them thrive among their sires,
but once they're settled in, my home's undone.

Still, every morning when I see one killed,
I see the family's elongate face
and wince at all the carnage I have willed
against an easily garrotted race.

Regret would be the name of what I feel.
It's nothing new. The world's awash in it.
We all want cards reshuffled — a fresh deal.
Without regrets life's nothing but warm spit.

WATCHING WATER

Follow with your eye the snowflake down,
a lightweight parachute the weight of light
until it masses, gathers miniscules
in billions and turns tall, a glacier.

And then it edges downhill like a train
that's just about, but grudgingly, to leave
a station where it stood and thought for years
with cars enough to belt the planet's waist.

And on, at regal pace, until the far
equator sends its emissaries of
the piercing sun, the love that kills, the warmth
unlocking all its cold solidity.

It calves and calves until it calves itself,
then goes to vapor where our eyesight ends.
All this we watch and say, "How beautiful!"
as if observing gladiators die.

THE RIGHTEOUS MAN

My mirrored face is not the face that's mine.
I'd never let pedestrians observe
my lower life, the dribble when I dine.

No doldrums! Let them see my verve.
They always keep what's worst and lose the best.
So may they keep the nothing, lose their nerve.

I scorn the tester, but I loathe the test,
for therein lies trespassing and offense.
I have full charity for all the rest:

for bossy matrons, for untidy gents,
for those who do not smile and nod hello,
for all these fools my charity's immense.

If only they would somehow deign bestow
such pure esteem on me, the world would glow.

A DIFFERENT BEGINNING

What if
instead of us poor primates
learning how to speak,
the squids already could,
rippling their chromatic sentences
while scooting like hovercrafts
across the California beaches,
setting up tilapia farms
among the bush lupine,
raising more articulate offspring
and discussing amid dinner
the reddening expense of colleges.

The youths would leave
the blood-soaked sand
of scales and tails of fish
to be with their friends,
occasionally causing an argument
between two Humboldt types,
and one entire family would be
wiped out just because it could be done.

I guess it doesn't make much difference
what assumptions you begin with.

EVERYTHING IS OTHERWISE

With all the things I've ever learned to do —
grout tile, teach literature, appreciate my wife —
I learned it just as health and age said, Stop.

And sometimes, maybe the most crucial times,
success was just beyond my fingertips,
something I'd have grasped if I hadn't fallen dead.

But when I think of Socrates, told to commit suicide;
Lao-Tzu, his wisdom confiscated as he left China;
Da Vinci who hardly ever finished anything;
Lincoln's lead payment for holding the nation together;
and Jeshua assassinated by the Jerusalem he loved;
I begin to see that nothing succeeds if it succeeds.

The Iliad is left to scholars who seek their own fame,
and Beowulf's stern syllables survive as a flashy film.
Give us all failure, and let it float away like a dead king.

Let me learn to respect my son's unpromising plans,
my daughter's disastrous choice of a husband,
and my neighbor's hatred of the things I say.

THE 20TH CENTURY

The Great War — that like a veteran rapist
went away and then returned for more —
hangs like a dark solidity over the era,
so disheartening that when it passed for good
our worship of our home became exaggerated
with babbling cyclopes showing idealized housewives
vacuuming in party dresses and frilly aprons.

Individualism huddled itself in drive-ins,
backyard barbecues and bedrooms for everyone.
We saw in our mirrors the best the world had known,
choosing our leaders singlehandedly, uncompromising,
proud of our humble status — our domed lunchbox,
patched working clothes, calloused hands and minds,
fumbling our way toward dynasties that died young.

We knew somewhere deep that the days of slaves
were going to end, so we began to find ways
for things to do our menial chores — clothes washers,
gas heaters, electric lights, cotton gins; and then
air conditioned, CD equipped, satellite-oriented
tractors selling for only $200,000 apiece,
and mostly unrepairable. But best of all was
the car, with radio and heater, an enclosed living
room that took its occupants elsewhere at a
speed that shamed horses and cheetahs,
selecting only a small percentage of lives as pay.

When it ended, we thought the world was ending,
and we looked to the future like Irish villagers
looking forward to the next Viking raid.
Now we look back on it with nostalgic fondness,
like remembering Mussolini's punctual trains.

RISING AGAIN

Deliberate and slow, in its good time,
a feeble tree root will subvert the mass
of concrete sidewalk and, turned hard as brass,
will make it, as though feathers, rise and climb;

so I, in my ignoble naiveté,
pulled down my humbler head and lifted high
our nine-month marvel, just a fraction shy
of buildings' heft, to animate our clay.

The time was swelling; it was ebbing too;
and all among the ocean's fertile span.
Not only did my lust give rise to you,
it gave rise to a more prospective man.

So when we breathe no more, we will inspire
him with such breath as lends him our desire.

3. The world beside us

THE WOLF PEOPLE

The sun had dried the ground.
You could not step without a puff of dust.
Jays screeched at the heat.
We with garbage for the midden
where the gray wolves swarmed,
picking through our leavings,
keeping an eye alert for us.

What if they did not skulk away?
What if they got used to us?
Would they stay and leap for the orts in our hands?
Whose midden would it be then?
I had seen them across the canyon eating an elk calf,
tearing off pieces before it died.
Would that be one of the People?

They turned again, slowly. Had it begun?
I dumped my basket on the pile
and that is when I saw the eyes
two tents away, staring at us. A young one.

My brother had the snake in him,
one cousin the otter, another the beaver.
It was time for me. Was wolf my tutam?

Day and days I took the garbage,
at first asking, then grabbing it before the others.
I had to fight Kamput to do it.

All the People were watching me
walk among the wolves.
One day I put down a bone, a little meat still on.
A gray wolf came slow, slow, grabbed it and ran.
I knew then. Klusit was my real name, Gray Wolf.

Now the hair leaves my head,
grows from my stretching ears, grows gray.
Now the People have wolves
among the tents, because of me.

I have taken into me the wolves' ways —
fighting, feeding, playing, breeding.
Now the People come to me when they need a pup.
Now when the Other Kind attack
the wolves help us and the Other People run.

I walk among the tents.
Whatever I look at, soon it is near my tent flap —
hatchets, knives, ropes, wives.
I wake, I walk out past my gift, climb to the peak,
hold up my empty hands to show I am unarmed
and I chant thanks to the Great Wolf above.

It will be warm today. It will be good.

ANIMAL SCRIPT

It is not true that only we can write.
The fox who steps so gingerly inscribes
his name in vulpine letters; and the elk
writes Elk across the paper we call snow.

Even the horse, subservience aside,
wears on his feet four broken signet rings
to signify, when all four feet are glue,
that he was royal once, and led his kin
to flourish on the Mongol steppes, but then
was vanquished by a weaker sort of beast,
a primate, a savannah breed too sly
for trials of brute strength, persistent too,
who nailed these iron styli to his hooves,
assigning him to write his servanthood
upon that primal page, the dust of Earth.

TRIPTYCH

An anna hummingbird rests content
for a few seconds on a fuchsia branch
before glimmering off to find other
generous blossoms or, it may be,
a hapless spider or mosquito.

Meanwhile seven hundred miles away
the earth heaves and blows
like a woman about to give birth.
And like the human birth
the geologic one may eject
anything from a trickle of slaver
to a gigantic mass murderer.

Of what importance then is it
when an experimental aircraft,
single-winged, faster than any known,
slices high across a gray sky,
turns and runs back the way it came,
then does a vertical loop and crashes,
bouncing along in decreasing explosions,
finally stopping so that we can hear
a voice say, "Get me to a place
where I can move"?

BARN

Built of black oak post and lintel,
dirt floor soaked in the piss and dung
of cows, geese, horses, sheep and dogs,
to say nothing of mice and a clan of cats,
it had stood undaunted for a century
when the winds and snows broke its back.

Now it leans, a matriarch on her cane,
trusted only by the mice and owls.
Does it hold some shape that it recalls,
or are we its memory, flitting like birds?

Whichever is true, the recollection fades,
like everything below the moon's cold smile.

TRADING AND BREEDING

Two red books on a table, volumes 1 and 2,
are the perfect counterbalance to acres of
green trees for our daily walk.
There the redwoods and fungi have learned
how to form an actual community, like ancient
Mediterraneans trading via a lingua franca
born of necessity and a conditional trust.

Just as eastern whitetails and western mule
deer interbreed near their territorial borders,
or as Leander took on the wild Hellespont
to reach Hero in her outlandish costume,
so the body itself revolts at too much inbreeding,
making the stupidity of provincialism obvious.

Terminal patriots are fossilized in their
proto-love, and family affection lives on
in the brain stem, where reptiles
had what served them for a thought.
Love is a seed that either expands or rots.

MONKEY SEE, MONKEY DO

"In all likelihood, the natives who made the trail
were animals, followed, in time, by people."
~*John McPhee*

Funny how the everted spine of an eoturtle
became a soldier's or construction worker's helmet;
the matted hair of a bison's pelt became
a coat, a cape, a blanket, a pair of leggings;
the raven's nest became a cozy bed;
the termite's mound, overlaid by the beaver's dam,
was transformed into huts, homes and palaces,
turreted, with intersecting logs or stones — mud,
cement or nails attaching them as a single thing.

We are, after all, the imitative animal,
monkey seeing its forbears do the darnedest things,
and monkey doing with a difference, a brain twist.
How we stand on the shoulders of alligators,
bees and swallows; how we intelligently envy
the quetzalcoatl and the hummingbird, the gorilla's
one-night nest, the parasitic wasp's laying
its eggs in someone else's nest, teaching us
to raise our children in the richest of economies.

EXPOSED

Away from city lights, from fog or smog,
those cosmic glints seem brighter and more real.
It's then we see how scant a shield we have
from endless falling, and how little chance
we'd have of ever landing anywhere.

Now think of those poor hypocrites who said
that Galileo had it wrong: "If earth
rotated (God forbid!), we'd be thrown off
this naked sphere. And yet we stand, unmoved."

They saw one-half the case alone — the fright —
while Galileo wanted only facts.
And what would you or I reply if we
were faced with choosing peace or frightful truth?

MAY IN THE GARDEN

Late spring, and the roses open their eyes.
Peonies are almost done, daffodils gone,
but larkspurs squander their deep blue
on anyone in view. Pansies reveal their
thoughts in mute parables with none
of the genetic shyness violets bear; and the
crabapple tree unleashes its orchestra with
an etude of one pink note. The varied
thrush offers his biography in a whistle
as white-faced chickadees arrow from
feeder to nest with seed-packed crops.
Dahlias are still only tentative leaves,
waiting for fewer distractions, a bare stage;
chrysanthemums a promise; asters legend.

EXTENSIONS OF THE BODY

In the beginning there were fingernails
for clawing and teeth for biting,
natural weapons, the fetuses of tools.
Not until they were given birth as stone,
soon knapped into knives, were they tools,
keen extensions of the body's hardnesses.

But for hunting and war this was too close,
too personal and vulnerable, so someone
stuck it on the end of a branch, and
the spear appeared. At first it was held
for jabbing, then it was thrown, followed
by running away. There was, for a time,
the atlatl, but it was hard to learn.

Somewhere, maybe on the Mongol steppes,
a genius made a bow, another branch,
but this time with sinew for a string.
He tried to capture the branch's strength,
and with its length, the string around
the spear, make a super-atlatl. Easy.
But an utter failure. It took his sister
to make a miniature spear, a toy really.
And this, with a tail of feathers (frailty)
and an unobtrusive notch (the feminine),
became archery. It took the dust of
Chinese fireworks to create the latest
transformation, but there is some hope
for lasers.

ITADAKIMASU*

I have received water, flowing and pooled, salt and fresh,
> cold and hot; wind off the ocean, among the trees,
> over wheat fields; wool for warmth.

I am grateful for these, and for the many-touching octopi,
> the common beauty of oleanders, tough-limbed
> oaks, lithe ocelots, leather-skinned oranges, and
> pungent onions.

About me lie perch from farm ponds, peppers and parsnips,
> potatoes and tellicherry peppercorns, pork and
> peaches, paprika, together with the sweet sadness
> of Pachelbel.

I have been given air to breathe, alders leafing out in spring,
> crisp apples, deep-flavored apricots, and the shield-
> like leaves of aspidistras.

Grapes and goldfinches, garlic and grass are in my treasury;
> jackrabbits and jays, ginger and juncos have come
> to me as gifts.

I am inebriated on biscuits and bass, bread and bears,
> bicycles and barracudas, on basil and brass.

Clouds and rainfall, snow and sleet, sunshine and darkness
> are my blessings, as are moonlight and firelight,
> starlight and candlelight.

I have been awarded Mozart and Bach, Verdi and Puccini,
> Homer and Shakespeare, Thomas More and Martin
> Luther, Herbert and Donne.

I have received from on high appreciative dogs and dignified
> housecats, deer and raccoons, chickens and grosbeaks,
> friendship and children, fuchsias and dahlias, soil,
> stone and steel.

May I never be ungrateful for any shelter, any mouthful of
> food or sip of water, any friendly gesture, any offer
> of help, any touch of understanding.

Japanese: "I have received from on high."

4. portraits

ARTHUR ON LANCELOT

Of course I knew. What choice was there for me?
It was to lose him from my table, my ablest knight,
or lose a modicum of honor in the whisperings,
a trifle by comparison. Besides, he was my friend,
which counterbalanced my resentment
when I pictured them at tossing on her bed,
her joyous cries more heartfelt than
she sighed for my more nobly-driven thrusts.

And I had winked at other couplings
in strange beds, one knight substituting for another,
to keep a semblance of the peace.
A king must leave aside these boyish frisks
to give his thought of statecraft better weight.
I had the table fashioned round to say
that every man was knight, and each had say,
the king reserved to give the final say.
How could I move more fiercely at my own
concern than at another's?
And yet, from that day that I knew, her face was
maculate, her voice a rasp, her hands a milkmaid's.
I took no longer sprightly to her bed.
Therein lay the poison that assassinated all.

THE NURSE IN THE ODYSSEY

Yes, nursed him I did when he was but a lad,
but when his teeth got sprouted, put my dugs away.
"No more," I said, and land, did he blubber.
(My husband said, "Good chance," and had a sup.)
Went off to his uncle's for to learn manhood,
got a boar's tusk in his leg what took many
a gathering of simples to close it on the blood.

Then was that doxy Helen gone with Paris,
Left her daughter and husband away behind
for the high life in Priam's land, they say.
So all the fit Achaeans supposed to go
and get her back, with all her "charms,"
to decency. Bah, say I, let her highness choke
on cates. She's worth not one Greek boy
speared through and left to die on foreign sand.

But go he did, for trickery won't always work,
even if your name is known for it — Odysseus.
And stayed away ten year, and then another ten
when all the others sat in settles by the fire.
And she, poor soul, aweaving and ataking out
to keep the heated suitors all at bay.

Comes one, a beggar don't you know, in rags
and begs to talk to her in private-like.
Tells her Odysseus is living and is near.
She's on her guard for just such lies, but
tells me bathe the fellow, as custom is.
I do, and there's the scar the boar's tusk left.
The rest is royalty. I have no more to say.

CASUAL CHIC

Uncle Frank would take a bath each day,
then shave and rinse his facial hairs away.
In natty suit, white shirt and a silk tie,
he'd walk out like a man who'll never die,
but live forever in a posh hotel.
The girls adored his manly, wholesome smell.

But then a Nazi with a curt mustache
began to turn his scapegoats into ash,
so Uncle Frank put off his natty suit
and donned some clothes more proper to dispute.
In olive drab, and in a Sherman tank,
he charged the Bulge, and there went Uncle Frank.

I think of him, a redhead on his arm,
a dandy who could never come to harm,
evaporated in a flash of Tiger fire,
the joy of style undone upon the pyre
of war's disorder, anger's deshabille,
the turning of the ages' wobbling wheel.

APPLES ON SNOW

Now that he's sleepy, he recalls
the day he turned ten
and his father allowed him to go
along on a rabbit hunt
in an old apple orchard
miles from the city.
The trees stood black
and hung with red apples.
The ground was blank with snow
except for a few blood drops of apples.
He'd brought his Red Ryder bb gun,
mostly to have something manly to carry,
but when his father made a pile of snow
and handed him his Browning 12-gauge,
he didn't say no.
He held the wobbling, hump-backed gun,
jerked the trigger, and the white hill
turned into the gray sky,
a piece of magic,
a rite survived.

On the way home,
dead rabbits in the trunk
of his father's '46 Packard Clipper,
he held a live one on his lap,
a shocked souvenir of his
success in becoming worthy
of respect from adults.

It quivered non-stop,
excreting a series
of pea-sized dry pellets.
Then it died
along with his plans
for world fame.
Through the speeding window

the fallen apples
turned as dark as their parent trees,
and he almost as disillusioned
and hungry for praise as his father,
until he awoke years later
enough to think it through.

AUTO BIOGRAPHY

Relieved of sheep-shank travel
and the butt-thumping of a donkey-cart,
the jam-packed steamship
then the locomotive carried them
to New York, Kansas City, San Francisco,
Brazil and Argentina where
they planted themselves as stonemasons,
farmers, auto mechanics, owners of
mom-and-pop grocery stores.

Sometimes it was a move to avoid
the sbirri back home;
at others it created clashes
with the cops of the new world, new life.
But always it was an uprooting,
and then a fervid try at
sinking new roots, a new start, hardly ever
with a thought to the new direction
except to make money, save it,
live in a big house and drive a big car,
something you could, in a daydream,
take back to Ragusa, to Sicily,
and drive the cramped streets while
looking straight ahead all of the time
as if you were thinking of something else.

THIS IS NOT A MARRIAGE

Now in early morning's tentative light
it all begins to come clear —
the spoons in their drawer slots,
the flashlight where it might be needed,
my wife still asleep in our bed.

We moved here from 7 climates away
not knowing if our transplanted needs
could accept the acid soil and the timid sun.
But in a week the house began to live,
its faucets standing like Renaissance servants
ready to pour out the water of many uses,
the electric outlets eager to inspire tools,
the heating here for the easy asking.

Taken alone, all this is not a marriage,
but begun in such a place,
like a plant in the loam of our lust,
it aspires to more, and it finds more as it rises
into the air, the light, the admiration.

We water it with our losses, prune it
lightly with our respect for its future,
and cater to its needs with our own need
for mercy projected onto it as a friend.

FISHING SIMPLIFIED

The moonlight kindles every ripple to
a minnow or a meal.
But still I fish down deep
for lunkers that are lying somnolent.

The water tongues my jon boat like a hound
that laps the weathered wood.
How will I know a bite?
A twitch, a smidgeon more than ripples do.

The moon peers from behind a willow now,
its light a little dimmed.
I doze. And then my line,
my rod and reel, are yanked from my lax hand

and I am left with just a boat and oars,
the sequins from moonlight,
and peace despite the night.

THE GOOD LIFE

He told me he was grateful he'd been born
to parents who could barely pay the rent.
The smells of sewage as you climbed the stairs
or burning garbage on a summer day,
the shattered glass in hamburger that killed
the barking dog in two days' agony,
the ice man with his tongs and pee-soaked pants,
the hardly spoken prayer for privacy,
all wakened in his youth an appetite
for what was only at the city's edge —
the wide-spaced houses and the simple air.

In time, the extra bedroom lined with books,
and roses all along the garden paths,
he'd leave to lecture on what pleased him best,
returning to write sonnets on the scent
of roses on the springtime's warming air.

AGED

Forty years it had been since we
left the Green Berets. Now he puffed
toward me across the lawn, the
toned and hardened warrior of his body in
retreat from a youthful self-confidence to —
as it turned out — sagging sincerity.

We found chairs and a cocktail table,
he smoking Camels, I a Peterson pipe,
and drank black label on the rocks.
It hasn't left me yet how rotund
he'd become. I of course was too,
but that's because of cortizone.

He paces himself now,
accepting his softening abilities
as he must, a thing we never thought of
when we climbed, jumped, swam,
chopped, chased, marched all night,
then showered, dressed and went on dates.

Now we sat and drank and smoked.
Even our sentences were hard to finish —
correction, his sentences.

THE MISER'S DEADLINE

He never paid until the walls closed in
and threatened jail, embarrassment or death.
There was a hole under the Christmas tree
where his wife's present should have been,
until the Eve filled it with cologne from U-Totem;
he paid his fines just before the deputy arrived;
and when — driving mountain roads at night —
he finally realized he (and his family) might
die for lack of gasoline, he stopped near
a parked pickup, started draining its tank,
then heard the "shlack-shluck" of a shotgun.
He begged for his life, and the man let him go.
As he slid under the steering wheel, he stank.

And what was behind all this procrastination?
A thrill, that's what, the thrill of knowing the
ones were still in his billfold, of feeling them
against his buttock, the carnal ecstasy of
knowing no one could take it away from him.
Then the deadline came, and he didn't know it.

THANKSGIVING

The sound of pie crust being pounded
and the smell of turkey dressing in the oven;
a Mozart divertimento, together with
the early seed-and-bulb catalogs.

A labrador on the kitchen floor
being licked by the tomcat who soon
tires of it, bites the dog's cheeks,
getting no response to pain, and walks away.

The day's a medly of sun and clouds,
planks of sunlight touching on the denuded
clearing to be impregnated next spring
with daffodils, foxgloves, daisies, ranunculi.

At present it is all promises, only promises.
But how much better than no promise at all.
We take them into us like food, flourishing
on their insistence that life is unquenchable.

BEING ALIVE AND HAVING TO DIE

After surviving my first eviction
into fluorescent light and
the gonging of steel pans,
this oddity of space and motions
had hardly become custom
when I learned I would one day dissolve.

One said it would be final, terminal,
all there is to it.
Another said it was one more passage
like the Bering Straits —
a narrow gate into a wider world.
A third said nothing, just went on
chopping firewood, carrying water,
as the birds went on chittering.

5. Making Light of It

THE WOMAN WHO LIVED BACKWARDS

There was an old woman who lived in reverse:
She died in a crib and was born in a hearse.

In driving her car (in reverse gear of course),
She always made sure it was pushed by a horse.

Her garden grew tall with potatoes and peas,
So tall that their top leaves grew down to her knees.

She fizzled and sputtered when things were correct,
But whistled and hummed when her new car was wrecked.

The food she devoured (like ice cream and pork)
Refined her until she had legs like a stork.

She'd often set fistfuls of money on fire.
Guess what! The next day her bank balance was higher.

She read eighty books in the space of one summer,
And — wouldn't you know — in the fall she was dumber.

Her house was so spotless by noon every Friday
She brought in more trash just to make it more tidy.

She traveled each evening to where she'd been hired
And worked very hard so as not to be tired.

And then the next morning she'd hurry home fresher
To write a critique of her foe, M.C. Escher.

She turned on the light before going to bed,
Then slept with bare feet and a blanketed head.

She didn't get married but split in two pieces,
Then one of her went off to live with her nieces.

The other grew older till she was a baby.
And all of this story is partly true, maybe.

NASTY NICK & THE BANKER'S KINFOLK

Old Nasty Nick,
He never worked a lick,
Just settin on the porch the livelong day.
But when it came to courage,
Old Nick could stir the porridge.
They's many men would shiver when he'd say,
"A fight is jest another kind of play."

Now Miss Polly was right purty,
But as doves go she was dirty.
The one thing she demanded was her pay.
Banker Caswell he refused her.
It appeared that this amused her
For she shot him as her friends all heard her say,
"Hit's cash or you won't live no more to play."

Well the townfolk paid no mind,
And the sheriff acted blind,
But the banker's kinfolk set up for a fray.
They come in from everwheres
On their geldings and their mares.
Old Nick jest scratched and then I heard him say,
"This fight is jest another kind of play."

They was buck-n-ball and bullet,
So nobody seen him pull it
When Nick's Walker up and started in to neigh.
In a minute they was finished

And their kin right sore diminished,
As we saw when all the gunsmoke cleared away.
A fight for Nick was jest a kind of play.

Then Miss Polly she admired him.
If she could have, she'd of hired him,
But he told her as he chawed a piece of hay,
"Ain't no call to be so grateful.
Work to me is sorta hateful.
This shady porch is where I aim to stay.
Fightin now, that's jest my kind of play."

CONFESSION TO PROCLIVITIES

I have fallen in love with
the strong nuclear force constant,
which would be comforting, I suppose,
were it not for the fact that I am
equally weakened in the knees by
the weak nuclear force constant.

And I am congenial with
the velocity of light,
the average distance between galaxies
and the decay rate of protons.

If anything arouses my lust, it is
the polarity of the water molecule
in bed together with
the epoch for white dwarf binaries.

But I must confess to my most
peculiar idiosyncrasy of all:
my having become accustomed to
water's temperature of maximum density,
along with
the strength of the cosmic primordial
magnetic field,
the latter, in French, being called
le champ aimanté.

www.ingramcontent.com/pod-product-compliance
Lightning Source LLC
Chambersburg PA
CBHW022123040426
42450CB00006B/826